Advance praise for *How S*

I can only wish that a resource
was in my early years of educati
will prove invaluable to that demographic, as well as those more senior
but perplexed by the strident claims of those currently expounding evolutionary doctrine.

In my thirty-five years of experience as physicist, voluntary Christian educator, board member, and currently assistant pastor, I have wit-
nessed the faith of many young people being challenged by the alleged
conflict in understanding origins, and it is good that an effective tool in
countering these claims is going to be available.

—Gordon Wood, Ph.D.
National Research Council, Retired Physicist

[This book is] a helpful document… it provides a readable background
to the present state of affairs and although basic, it answers many typi-
cal questions relevant to believers… it more than serves the purposes…
It will be a useful foundation for our students to absorb.

—Wilf Hildebrandt, B.Min., M.T.S., Th.M., D.Th.
Dean of Education,
Summit Pacific College, British Columbia

[This book is] readable/easy to follow/not technical… I most enjoyed
the section on Christ Atonement, Fossil Evidences, and Genetic Evidences… this is a great work and I pray that believers are birthed out of
[reading] the publication of this work for His kingdom.

—Jonathan
Bible College Student, Senior Year

The booklet is a clear, concise presentation of the important issues
surrounding the question of origins. It is a ready resource for anyone
seeking to address or resolve the common points in the creation vs.
evolution discussion from a biblical perspective.

—Doug Stringer, B.A., M.A., D.Min.
Associate Pastor, City Church and Capital Biker's Church

As a high school science teacher for seventeen years (now retired), I find much to appreciate in this well-written booklet by experienced science educators John Byl and Tom Goss. The authors understand the scientific claims of the evolutionary worldview and they capably deconstruct them in the light of biblical truth. To thoughtful Christians, both young and older, I highly recommend the careful study of this booklet.

—Richard Peachey, B.Sc.
High School Science Teacher
Former Vice-President, Creation Science Association
of British Columbia

I really enjoyed the book... [especially] its simplicity in language and readability, its biblical use and support of arguments, very respectful tone for other views and opinions... it was more than I was expecting, too, as my brain doesn't always think scientifically... [This book on origins is like] the starting line for understanding our origins: it is an excellent introduction to the relationship between Scripture and Science... [The authors] respectfully engage the various views of origins without sacrificing the supremacy of Scripture. The perfect place to begin for all seekers of God's Truth... especially for Bible students and pastors.

—Terry
Bible College Graduate

There is probably not a single church leader these days that sends their students off to university confident of their readiness to meet the predictable challenges to their faith and their worldviews, especially when it comes to the creation-origins debate. This booklet is the help you need to help them and it takes away every excuse not to engage the student ministries and get them ready! Engage the whole church with it, for that matter!

—Terry Burns Sr., B.A., B.B.S., M.Ed., (cand.) D.Min.
Senior Pastor, Pembroke Pentecostal Tabernacle

HOW SHOULD CHRISTIANS APPROACH ORIGINS

JOHN BYL   **TOM GOSS**

ACKNOWLEDGMENTS

Many people made this booklet possible. Foremost, I (TG) thank my science course students at Summit Pacific College for their questions and inspiration. I thank all my colleagues at Summit who encouraged me, especially Roger Stronstad (for his friendship, and for his Foreword to the booklet), Wilf Hildebrandt, Dave Demchuk, Fred Fulford, and Rob McIntyre. We thank all our reviewers for their helpful suggestions, especially those who endorsed the booklet. We much appreciate the creativity and work done by Martin Murtonen on our cover design. Lastly, and truly important to us, we thank our wives, Linda and Margaret, for sharing our journey, and encouraging us, throughout this labor of love for the Lord.

HOW SHOULD CHRISTIANS APPROACH ORIGINS?
Copyright © 2015 by John Byl and Tom Goss

All rights reserved. Neither this publication nor any part of this publication may be reproduced or transmitted in any form or by any means, electronic or mechanical, including photocopying, recording or any information storage and retrieval system, without permission in writing from the author.

Scripture quotations are from the ESV® Bible (The Holy Bible, English Standard Version®), copyright © 2001 by Crossway, a publishing ministry of Good News Publishers. Used by permission. All rights reserved. Scripture quotations marked (NASB) taken from the New American Standard Bible®, Copyright © 1960, 1962, 1963, 1968, 1971, 1972, 1973, 1975, 1977, 1995 by The Lockman Foundation. Used by permission.

ISBN: 978-1-4866-1212-3 Printed in Canada

Word Alive Press
131 Cordite Road, Winnipeg, MB R3W 1S1
www.wordalivepress.ca

Cataloguing in Publication may be obtained through Library and Archives Canada

FOREWORD

As a badge of honor, evangelical Christians often identify themselves as "Bible-believers," in contrast to other Christians who, for example, do not believe that miracles can happen. At this point in the development of evangelical Christianity, however, many evangelical Christians have stopped reading the Bible they profess to follow. As a result, they may more aptly be classified as "Bible non-readers." This is sometimes followed by a further step, for "Bible non-readers" can quickly become "Bible non-believers." This is happening in the field of origins. Increasing numbers of so-called Bible-believers do not believe the biblical data about creation.

Properly understood, biblical creationism is a majestic and magnificent divine activity. It is the first biblical doctrine: *"In the beginning God created the heavens and the earth"* (Genesis 1:1, NASB). It is the first phase in redemption: *"In the beginning was the Word... All things came into being through Him"* (John 1:1, 3, NASB). Creation is a self-evident truth:

> *For since the creation of the world His invisible attributes, His eternal power and divine nature, have been clearly seen, being understood through what has been made, so that they are without excuse. (Romans 1:20, NASB)*

Therefore, God is to be worshipped, *"for [He] created all things, and because of [His] will they existed, and were created"* (Revelation 4:11, NASB). But because mankind does not acknowledge the God of the first creation (and redemption), there will be *"a new heaven and a new earth; for the first heaven and the first earth passed away..."* (Revelation 21:1, NASB). God is active in the world in many ways, but in one sense, the first thing God ever did was create, and the last thing He ever will do is create anew.

And so, Christians are faced with a dilemma: having believed that He is their Redeemer-God, can they now reject Him as their Creator-God? The Bible asserts that you can't consistently believe the one (redemption) without believing the other (creation). As it is written,

By faith we understand that the worlds were prepared by the word of God… And without faith it is impossible to please Him, for he who comes to God must believe that He is and that He is a rewarder of those who seek Him. (Hebrews 11:3, 6, NASB)

The question then is: how should Christians approach origins? A good place to start is this booklet by two university science professors well qualified to speak on the topic, namely John Byl and Tom Goss, whose title is that question. Their booklet is a guide for the bewildered, the confused, and/or the believer who needs help to understand the issues. This is an irenic, evenhanded, easily understood discussion. While one may not agree with everything that Byl and Goss write, this book about origins will prove to be of lasting worth.

—Dr. Roger Stronstad, Th.Dip., M.C.S., D.D., D.D.
Scholar in Residence, Summit Pacific College, British Columbia

1. INTRODUCTION

1.1 WHAT SHOULD CHRISTIANS BELIEVE ABOUT ORIGINS?

This booklet is addressed to Bible-believing Christians, including pastors, teachers, church leaders, and especially students, to help them examine the key issues around origins.

Until about two hundred years ago, most Christians believed that God created the world and everything in it from nothing in six days about six thousand years ago. The original creation was very good. Adam was miraculously created by God from dust, and Eve was created from Adam's side. Adam's fall into sin brought suffering, disease, and death into the world. All people descended from Adam and Eve.

This contrasts starkly with the account of mainstream science, backed by the majority of scientists, which alleges that everything originated and evolved by purely natural means from an initial big bang some fourteen billion years ago. As space expanded, energy was transformed into particles of matter, which subsequently formed into stars and planets. On at least one planet, simple life arose which evolved into more complex forms of life and eventually produced us modern humans.

How should Christians react to the story of origins as told by mainstream science? Should they modify the traditional position? Does it really matter what one believes about origins?

1.2 ARE THE BIBLE AND SCIENCE SEPARATE?

Some Christians believe that mainstream science's view of history does not contradict the Bible, but complements it. Regarding ancient history, science is said to tell us what happened (the what, when, and how) whereas the Bible gives us the deeper interpretation (the why and by whom). In this view, God exists and created the universe, but thereafter the universe unfolded according to purely natural laws.

Others hold that theology and science are two disciplines that have nothing in common, as advocated by the American Association for the Advancement of Science and by agnostic Stephen Gould's NOMA (Non-Overlapping Magisteria).[1] In this view, theology deals with spiritual matters, whereas science deals with nature matters.

However, such a clean separation of science and Christianity cannot be consistently maintained. For example, the all-important biblical gospel of our salvation through our Lord Jesus Christ is based on the historical reality of His birth, death, and resurrection from the dead. The central thrust of Christianity includes also the imminent return of Christ, the resurrection of all dead humans, their judgment, and, for believers, life everlasting on a renewed earth. All these supremely important matters are worldly space-time events.

Indeed, the biblical message is based on the reality of actual historical events. Hence, the Bible is concerned not only with the why and by whom, but also with matters of the what, when, and how.

1.3 IS THE CONFLICT REAL?

The mere fact that the Bible and science are both concerned with space-time history need not cause any conflict. Problems arise when scientists try to reconstruct history solely in terms of natural laws and events.

Biblical history includes accounts of miracles (events not explicable by natural laws) directly caused by supernatural agents such as God, angels, or demons. Indeed, the gospel is based on the great miracle of the resurrection of Jesus Christ from the dead. This supernatural event has always been a stumbling block to some academics (Acts 17:32 says, *"Now when they heard of the resurrection of the dead, some mocked."*). However, this miracle is central to the gospel of Jesus Christ. Paul writes that *"if Christ has not been raised, then our preaching is in vain and your faith is in vain"* (1 Corinthians 15:14).

---

1 Stephen Jay Gould, "Non-Overlapping Magisteria." *Natural History* 106 (March 1997): 16–22.

Genuine Christians must therefore believe in the past occurrence of at least one miracle.

1.4 CAN MIRACLES HAPPEN?

Some people believe that science has proven that biblical miracles—indeed, all miracles—are impossible. Thus, for example, theologian Hans Küng contends that the miracles in the Bible are merely metaphors, not actual historical events that break the laws of nature.[2]

Similarly, the famous New Testament scholar Rudolph Bultmann believed that the world operated according to purely natural causes and effects. He was convinced that science had proven there was no room for spiritual agents or supernatural causes. He rejected even the resurrection of Jesus as primitive nonsense.[3]

2. SCIENCE AND HISTORY

Has science really proven that miracles are impossible? Let's have a brief look at the nature of science.

2.1 WHAT DO WE MEAN BY SCIENCE?

Science, very broadly, is the systematic study of the physical world. As such, it is necessarily grounded in our observations of nature. The observed data are analyzed, using mathematics, for patterns, regularities, and laws.

Science also includes a more speculative, theoretical component. Scientists want to explain reality. Particular events are explained in terms of known physical laws, and these laws are in turn explained in terms of more fundamental concepts, principles, and theories. Thus,

---

2 Hans Küng, *The Beginning of All Things: Science and Religion* (Grand Rapids, MI: William B. Eerdmans Publishing Company, 2007), 153.

3 Rudolf Bultmann, *Jesus Christ and Mythology* (New York, NY: Charles Scribner's Sons, 1957), 16.

for example, our observations of planets suggest a law stating that all planets orbit their suns in elliptical orbits; these elliptical orbits are then explained in terms of a broader gravitational theory such as Newtonian mechanics or Einstein's general relativity.

Scientists hope to extrapolate or predict beyond their limited set of observational data to draw more general conclusions about the universe at large. This requires various assumptions about the nature of the universe.

2.2 SCIENCE AND MIRACLES

For example, it is commonly assumed that the laws of nature are uniform, that the physical laws observed here and now are valid universally throughout time and space. This is a convenient simplifying assumption.

Yet, it *is* an assumption. Logically, there is no reason why the currently observed natural laws should hold always and everywhere. Nor can there be any observational proof, since our actual observations are quite limited in time and space.

Also, there have been many eyewitness reports of miracles, both in the Bible and elsewhere in recorded history. To reject all these accounts as false requires the assumption of uniformity. G.K. Chesterton has aptly noted:

> *Somehow or other an extraordinary idea has arisen that the disbelievers in miracles consider them coldly and fairly, while believers in miracles accept them only in connection with some dogma. The fact is quite the other way. The believers in miracles accept them (rightly or wrongly) because they have evidence for them. The disbelievers in miracles deny them (rightly or wrongly) because they have a doctrine against them.[4]*

---

4 G.K. Chesterton, *Orthodoxy* (Garden City, NY: Image Books, 1959), 150.

2.3 OPERATIONAL AND HISTORICAL SCIENCE

Our origin is part of history, the study of past events. Since the distant past can no longer be directly observed, scientists try to reconstruct history by extrapolating from current observational data.

It is sometimes argued that it is inconsistent to use modern medicine and technology while rejecting evolution, since both are products of mainstream science. However, we must be careful to distinguish between two types of science: *operational* science and *historical* science.

1. Operational science is the experimental science done in the lab or in the field. It investigates repeatable events in the present. This concerns most of physics, chemistry, and biology, as well as observational geology, astronomy, and the like. It gives us all the science needed for technology, such as in developing smartphones, satellites, cars, planes, cures for diseases, and so on. It studies the present material reality and how it normally functions.

2. Historical science, on the other hand, is concerned with extrapolating from present observations to the distant, unobserved, and unrepeatable past. This includes various theories and explanations in archaeology, cosmology, historical geology, paleontology, biological evolutionary development, and so on.

These two types of science differ significantly:

1. Operational science aims to discover the universal laws by which nature generally operates, whereas historical science aims to establish ancient conditions or past causes. Operational science explains present events by reference to general laws, whereas historical science explains present events in terms of presumed past events.

2. Operational science calculates forward, deducing effects from causes, whereas historical science calculates

backwards, inferring past causes from present clues. One problem here is that more than one possible historical cause can give rise to the same effect. For example, in a murder trial, the prosecution and defense may present very different historical scenarios to explain the material evidence.

3. Operational science assumes methodological naturalism. Since it is concerned with what normally happens, in the absence of miracles, it is reasonable to consider only natural causes. Historical science, on the other hand, seeks to find what actually happened in the past. Constraining ourselves to natural causes amounts to metaphysical naturalism—the further assumption that no miracles have in fact happened in the past.[5]

The well-known evolutionist Ernst Mayr acknowledged,

Evolutionary biology, in contrast with physics and chemistry, is a historical science—the evolutionist attempts to explain events and processes that have already taken place. Laws and experiments are inappropriate techniques for the explication of such events and processes. Instead one constructs a historical narrative, consisting of a tentative reconstruction of the particular scenario that led to the events one is trying to explain.[6]

In short, the scientific know-how needed to make smartphones is much better established than, say, the claim that humans evolved from chimpanzees.

---

5 Stephen Meyer, *Signature in the Cell* (New York: NY, HarperCollins, 2009), 150–172.

6 Ernst Mayr, "Darwin's Influence on Modern Thought." *Scientific American*, November 24, 2009 (http://www.scientificamerican.com/article/darwins-influence-on-modern-thought/).

2.4 THE SCIENTIFIC IMPORTANCE OF OBSERVATIONS

Reliable observational data always trumps scientific theories. After all, scientific theories are constructed to *explain* the data. Therefore, scientific reconstructions of the past must conform to reliable historical records of past events. For example, if a lava flow in Hawaii is dated by radiometric methods to be more than one million years old, but is known via historical records to have formed in AD 1860, then the radiometric date would be deemed faulty.

A prime issue is whether or not the Bible contains reliable historical information. If so, such biblical data should constrain scientific explanations in the historical sciences.

2.5 UNDERPINNING MODERN SCIENCE: NATURALISM

Scientific conclusions about the past depend on our prior assumptions about the universe as a whole. These assumptions, in turn, reflect our worldview, our most basic notions regarding reality.

Mainstream science is currently controlled by naturalism. Naturalism's basic theme is that nature is self-sufficient; that is, it is independent of God. Nature, it is alleged, exists by itself, deriving all meaning and purpose from itself. Most naturalists are materialists, holding that everything in the universe evolved from an initial speck of matter-energy.

Naturalists aim to explain every aspect of life, even religion, in purely natural terms. Consider, for example, the reflections of the naturalist historian of science and evolutionary biology William Provine:

> *Evolutionary biology... tells us... that nature has no detectable purposive forces of any kind... There are no gods and no designing forces that are rationally detectable...*
>
> *There are no inherent moral or ethical laws...*
>
> *We must conclude that when we die, we die and that is the end of us... There is no hope of everlasting life...*

> *Free will… the freedom to make uncoerced and unpredictable choices among alternative possible courses of action, simply does not exist… the evolutionary process cannot produce a being that is truly free to make choices…*
>
> *The universe cares nothing for us… There is no ultimate meaning for humans.*[7]

Such is the somber creed of materialism.

Naturalist scientists reject the biblical account of history primarily because of their inherent bias against the supernatural. They reject the notion that the Bible is divinely inspired, as well as any miracles the Bible relates.

Of course, not all mainstream scientists are naturalists. Scientists of many faiths participate in mainstream science, including Christians. Nevertheless, they may do so only if they follow naturalist rules. Christians may privately believe in God and His Word, but no reference to these may be made while taking part in mainstream science.

Christians are not anti-science. They do not dispute operational science, the experimental science done in the lab or in the field, and the empirical science needed for technology. Nor do Christians dispute reliable scientific observations. At issue are those claims of mainstream historical science that contradict biblical history. Bible-believing Christians will insist that viable scientific explanations of the past should conform to the biblical account of history.

Thus, although most Christian scientists work within mainstream science, a small minority have chosen to do their own Bible-based science (often called "creation science"). The choice is between historical science as done within a biblical worldview, where scientific theories are bounded by biblical truths, or as done within a naturalist worldview, where miracles are banned.

---

7 William Provine, "Progress in Evolution and Meaning of Life," in *Evolutionary Progress*, M.H. Nitecki, ed. (Chicago, IL: University of Chicago Press, 1988), 47–74.

3. THE CHRISTIAN WORLDVIEW

A Christian worldview has a number of beliefs pertinent to our discussion.

3.1 GOD IS THE ULTIMATE REALITY

Central to the Christian worldview is belief in a sovereign, all-knowing, good, and infinite tri-personal God: the Father, the Son Jesus Christ, and the Holy Spirit. God is self-sufficient, dependent on nothing beyond Himself. He is the ultimate cause of everything else. God transcends all His creatures. He is distinct from His creation, and He is *"over all"* (Romans 9:5). Thus, Christians view reality as much more than nature.

3.2 GOD IS TRUTH

Christians believe that God has revealed truth to us through His written Word, the Bible. Since God is all-knowing, the Bible should be considered authoritative in all that it affirms. To minimize human distortion in reading the Bible, we need clear rules for proper biblical interpretation. Two such rules, stressed by the Reformers, are:

1. The natural sense. We should interpret the Bible in its obvious, plain sense, taking context into account, unless internal evidence indicates otherwise.
2. Scripture interprets Scripture. The more clear passages shed light on the less clear passages. We must read the Bible on its own terms, letting the exegetical chips fall where they may.

A Christian theory of knowledge thus takes into account not only observational data and logic (including mathematics), but also biblical teaching. Viable scientific theories, as human constructs, should be consistent with all three of these.

3.3 THE UNIVERSE DEPENDS ENTIRELY ON GOD

God, through His Son,[8] created the entire universe, and all it contains, out of nothing. *"In the beginning, God created the heavens and the earth"* (Genesis 1:1) implies that the universe had a beginning in time, being created by God. And *"by faith we understand that the universe was created by the word of God, so that what is seen was not made out of things that are visible"* (Hebrews 11:3).

God, through His Son, is also the cause of its continuous existence: *"and he [Jesus Christ] upholds the universe by the word of his power"* (Hebrews 1:3). Without God's continual upholding Word, the universe would cease to exist. No creature can act independently of God's sustaining power.

The created universe consists not only of the observed physical universe, but includes also the highest heaven, the dwelling place of angels and the souls of departed saints, where Christ sits on the throne with His Father (Revelation 3:21). Since Christ has a physical body, this heaven has a physical aspect. However, since it is normally invisible to us, it is beyond scientific investigation. Science then can deal with only a small portion of the total universe.

3.4 GOD HAS A GLORIOUS PLAN

According to the Bible, history unfolds exactly in accordance with God's plan, established before the foundation of the world. Consider, for example, these texts:

> *...who works all things according to the counsel of his will...* (Ephesians 1:11)

> *...to do whatever your hand and your plan had predestined...* (Acts 4:28)

---

8 For example, see Colossians 1:15–17, John 1:1–3, and Ephesians 3:9.

...this Jesus, delivered up according to the definite plan and fore-knowledge of God... (Acts 2:23)

God is sovereign over history; nothing happens by chance. This includes even minor details, such as sparrows and hairs (Matthew 10:29–30). Every creature and every event has its purpose as part of God's plan.

The chosen plan of universal history is that which best fulfills God's purpose, which is to display His glory. God's glory is a basic theme of the Bible:

...all the earth shall be filled with the glory of the Lord... (Numbers 14:21)

For from him and through him and to him are all things. To him be glory forever. (Romans 11:36)

Some aspects of God's glory are displayed in the world:

The heavens declare the glory of God, and the sky above proclaims his handiwork. (Psalm 19:1)

3.5 MAN WAS CREATED TO BE GOD'S STEWARD

Man was created in the image of God (Genesis 1:27), upright and good (Ephesians 4:24), to serve God. But Adam rebelled and fell into sin. Thereafter, Adam and his offspring were wholly inclined to reject God and to do evil (Romans 3:9–19). Only through the redeeming work of Christ can we be saved. Even then, sinners can be saved only through the working of the Holy Spirit in their hearts, by the grace of God (Ephesians 2:8–9).

3.6 CHRISTIANITY AND MIRACLES

God generally upholds the universe from one moment to the next in accordance with the properties He has assigned to all creation. The moon, for example, orbits the earth in accordance with its gravitational character, animals follow their specific instincts, humans act according to their individual characters, and so on.

The regularity of nature is the result of God's faithfulness. He has made a covenant with His creation so that summer and winter, day and night, will not cease as long as the earth exists (Genesis 8:22; 9:11–12; Jeremiah 33:25). He has set bounds for all of His creation (Job 38–41; Acts 17:26). Hence, we can generally expect nature to be uniform. This makes it possible for us to plan our lives and conduct operational science.

However, the observed natural laws are only descriptive of how God typically runs the universe, not prescriptive of what must happen. God is free to act in new ways, even to transform the entire world after the second coming of Jesus Christ.

Thus, the uniformity of nature is not absolute. Sometimes God may act differently. Miracles are not divine interventions in a world that otherwise runs by itself. As we just saw, the world must at all times be sustained by God. Hence, miracles are less regular manifestations of God's will. Likewise, natural laws are not rigid rules but rather the more regular manifestations of God's will.

Moreover, we must also acknowledge the physical effect of spiritual agents, such as angels and demons, who can cause physical effects (2 Samuel 24:15–17; 2 Kings 19:35).

Thus, the Christian worldview, with its allowance for miracles and spiritual agents, entails that not all natural events have natural explanations.

3.7 SCIENCE AND CHRISTIANITY

Historically, the development of science owed much to Christianity.

The notion that the world was created by a rational God according to a plan suggested that it had order and purpose. Since man was created in the image of God, it was deemed possible that man could discern the structure of the universe. The cultural mandate, which appointed man to be God's steward over creation (Genesis 1:28), provided motivation for studying nature and applying that study towards practical ends, glorifying God for His wisdom and goodness.

It is often claimed that Genesis reflects faulty ancient cosmology, such as a flat earth covered by a solid dome. Such assertions have been soundly refuted.[9] The notion that early Christians believed the earth to be flat is a modern myth.[10]

Many founders of science were devout Christians (e.g., Copernicus, Galileo, Bacon, Kepler, Boyle, Newton, Faraday, Mendel, Pasteur, Maxwell). Scientific enterprise significantly advanced in the West in the sixteenth to eighteenth centuries, led by many outstanding discoveries by Christians.[11] The claim that creationists would undermine the advancement of science is simply unsupported by history.

Nevertheless, their successors gradually came to see God as unnecessary. By the nineteenth century, many scientists viewed science as the only means of acquiring truth about the world. Everything was to be explained in terms of purely natural processes. God was either denied or marginalized.

What about the seventeenth-century controversy between Galileo and his church about the motion of the earth? Did science disprove the biblical notion of a fixed earth? No. Science can deal only with relative motion. One's choice of an absolute standard of rest must be based on extra-scientific considerations, such as philosophical or theological factors. A geocentric biblical frame of reference is thus beyond any scientific disproof.[12]

Further, God's creation is much larger than the observable universe. It encompasses also the vast, spatial heaven where God and His

---

9 Noel K. Weeks, "Cosmology in Historical Context." *Westminster Theological Journal* 68 (2006): 283–93.

10 J.B. Russell, *Inventing the Flat Earth: Columbus & Modern Historians* (Westport, CT: Praeger, 1991).

11 See list of past Christian/creation scientists at www.creation.com/creation-scientists.

12 George Murphy, "Does the Earth Move?" *Perspectives in Science and Christian Faith* 63 (June 2011): 283–293.

angels reside. The ultimate focal point of the entire creation is arguably God's heavenly throne. Perhaps the earth is fixed in regards to this divine standard of rest (e.g., Isaiah 66:1).[13] The earth is certainly central to God's purposes; this is where Christ became incarnate, and where He will return to reign in the New Jerusalem (Revelation 21–22).

4. THE BIBLICAL ADAM VERSUS EVOLUTION

With the departure of the Creator, a theory such as evolution was needed to provide a naturalistic explanation of the origin of the various forms of life on earth.

To what extent should a Christian accept evolution? Small changes within a species (so-called microevolution) are not a problem. This can be observed to happen in the laboratory. At issue is whether large-scale evolution, from one species to another (macroevolution), has occurred in the past, and whether all life on earth has evolved from the first living cell (common ancestry). One major defect in naturalistic evolution is that no plausible process has yet been found that could produce even the simplest cell (which is amazingly complex). Scientists are as far as ever from creating life in the laboratory. How then did life ever get started?

A further problem is that macroevolution has never been observed to happen. Biologist Richard Lenski has an ongoing experiment on the *Escherichia coli* (*E. coli*). This is a simple single-celled bacterium with a generation time of only seventeen minutes. Starting in 1988, Lenski observed over sixty thousand generations of *E. coli*. He noted some changes in cell size, genetic makeup, and adaptations. But nothing substantially different was ever produced; *E. coli* cells always remained *E. coli* cells.[14]

---

13 John Byl, "A Moving Earth?" *Bylogos*. July 18, 2011 (http://bylogos.blogspot.ca/2011/07/moving-earth.html).

14 J.W. Fox and R.E. Lenski, "From Here to Eternity—The Theory and Practice of a Really Long Experiment." *PLoS Biology*, June 23, 2015 (http://journals.plos.org/plosbiology/article?id=10.1371/journal.pbio.1002185).

Our prime concern is the question of human evolution. According to mainstream science, humans evolved from ape-like ancestors a few million years ago, with a population size that was never smaller than ten thousand. This clashes with the biblical account, where all humans descend from an initial pair: Adam was created directly by God of dust from the ground, and Eve from the side of Adam.

In response, many Christians now question whether the biblical Adam really existed. Some, such as geneticist Francis Collins, fully endorse the current mainstream evolutionary view of origins and find no place for an historical Adam.[15] Theologian Peter Enns takes Genesis 1–3 to be symbolic, an allegory concerning the origin of Israel rather than of all humanity; Adam is reduced to a metaphor for Israel.[16] Denis Lamoureux believes that real history in the Bible begins around Genesis 12, with Abraham; Adam merely serves as the archetype for every man.[17] Theologian Amos Yong takes Adam to refer collectively to the first self-aware hominids.[18]

Others, such as Pastor Timothy Keller[19] and theologian John H. Walton,[20] seeking to accommodate evolution, affirm that Adam and Eve were historical individuals, but had animal ancestors and were part

15 Francis S. Collins, *The Language of God: A Scientist Presents Evidence for Belief* (New York, NY: Simon and Schuster, 2006), 207.

16 Peter Enns, *The Evolution of Adam: What the Bible Does and Doesn't Say about Human Origins* (Ada, MI: Brazos Press, 2012).

17 Denis O. Lamoureux, "No Historical Adam: Evolutionary Creation View," in *Four Views on the Historical Adam*, M. Barrett and A.B. Caneday, eds. (Grand Rapids, MI: Zondervan, 2013).

18 Amos Yong, *Theology and Down Syndrome* (Waco, TX: Baylor University Press, 2007), 322.

19 Timothy Keller, "Creation, Evolution and Christian Laypeople." *BioLogos* (August 2010), 12. He said that Adam and Eve "were products of evolution and given the image and breath of God."

20 John H. Walton, "A Historical Adam: Archetypal Creation View," in *Four Views on the Historical Adam*, M. Barrett and A.B. Caneday, eds. (Grand Rapids, MI: Zondervan, 2013).

of a larger population—perhaps they were chiefs or representatives of the tribe.

So should a Christian believe in a modified version of evolution, where God perhaps intervenes at critical points, such as endowing man with a soul? Many Christians believe this to be a viable option. Such a position is often called theistic evolution, or evolutionary creation.

4.1 WHAT DOES THE BIBLE SAY?

Did Adam and Eve really exist?

The Genesis account of Adam and Eve was accepted as accurate history by all the church fathers, the reformers Luther and Calvin, as well as the vast majority of Christians until recent challenges from naturalistic science.

Indeed, Genesis presents itself as history. Its style is narrative prose, not poetry. Throughout Genesis we find the phrase *"these are the generations of"* eleven times, starting at Genesis 2:4. Further, the Bible, whenever it elsewhere refers to Genesis 1–11, always takes it in its obvious, plain sense, as a record of historical events.

Due to some similarities between Genesis 1–11 and various myths of the ancient near east (ANE), it is sometimes alleged that Genesis contains modified ANE myths, and therefore is not historically reliable. However, from the biblical perspective, the ANE societies shared a common heritage from Noah, and thus their myths are merely distortions of the true record preserved in Genesis.

What does Genesis say? We read:

When... there was no man to work the ground... the Lord God formed the man of dust from the ground and breathed into his nostrils the breath of life, and the man became a living creature... Then the Lord God said, "It is not good that the man should be alone."... The man gave names to... every beast of the field. But for Adam there was not found a helper fit for him... And the rib that the Lord God had taken from the man he made into a woman... The man called his wife's name Eve, because she was the mother of all living. (Genesis 2:5, 8, 18, 20; 3:20)

The text says that *"the man became a living creature,"* not that *"the living creature became a man."* Adam was thus clearly the first man, created from inanimate dust to which he returns at death (Genesis 3:19).

Eve, too, was formed miraculously from Adam's side. They were each unique. Adam was alone, in need of a helpmate (Genesis 2:18); there were no other humans, no other animals *"fit for him."* If Adam had parents, one of the other creatures would have been close to him. Hence, there were no pre-Adamites or co-Adamites.

The genealogies of Genesis 5, 1 Chronicles 1, and Luke 3 all find their first parent in Adam. The historicity of Adam is presumed in Jesus' teaching on marriage (Matthew 19:4–6), Jude's reference to Adam (Jude 14), and Paul's assertion that Adam was formed first, then Eve (1 Corinthians 11:8–9, 1 Timothy 2:13). Most importantly, Paul links the historical Adam with redemption through Christ (Romans 5:12–19; 1 Corinthians 15:20–23, 42–49; Acts 17).

We can summarize the biblical teaching about Adam and Eve:

1. Adam and Eve were created from the beginning of creation (Mark 10:16).
2. Adam and Eve were real historical people, the first humans (Genesis 2).
3. Adam was directly created by God, and Eve from Adam (Genesis 2).
4. They had no animal ancestors (Genesis 2).
5. All other humans descended from Adam (Genesis 3:20, Acts 17:26).
6. Adam and Eve were created in the image of God (Genesis 1); their physical death was their punishment for sin (Genesis 3; Romans 5).
7. Adam and Eve had sophisticated language, were intelligent, were clothed (Genesis 3:21), had domesticated

sheep and grain, and their immediate children founded cities (Genesis 4). Adam fathered Seth at 130 years, and lived for 930 years (Genesis 5).

4.2 IMPLICATIONS OF QUESTIONING THE BIBLICAL ADAM

Biblical authority. One major consequence of questioning the biblical Adam is biblical authority. Were Jesus, Moses, Matthew, Mark, Luke, Jude, and Paul all wrong? Can we no longer trust the Bible? Peter Enns believes that Paul was mistaken about Adam. He says that Paul was a man of his time regarding his knowledge of origins, but that this error about Adam does not affect Paul's theological message.[21]

The origin of sin. However, demoting Adam to a metaphor, or tribal chief, does have deep theological implications. This was spelled out by Daniel Harlow[22] and John Schneider,[23] professors at Calvin College.

According to the Bible, man was created good but fell into sin due to his own willful choice. Thereafter, all humans inherited Adam's sinful disposition via biological reproduction (the doctrine of original sin). Adam is thus responsible for sin and evil. If Adam was merely a chief or representative of several thousand upright people, it is difficult to see how Adam's fallen nature would be transmitted to all his contemporaries. Moreover, if humans evolved, they could not have been originally upright. Our sinfulness and selfishness are then due not to an historical fall, but rather to our evolutionary heritage. Man was never free of sin or evil; selfishness was needed for survival. God, creating through evolution, is then responsible for human sin and evil.

---

21 Peter Enns, *The Evolution of Adam: What the Bible Does and Doesn't Say about Human Origins* (Ada, MI: Brazos Press, 2012).

22 Daniel C. Harlow, "After Adam: Reading Genesis in an Age of Evolutionary Science." *Perspectives on Science and Christian Faith* 62 (2010): 191–195.

23 John R. Schneider: "Recent Genetic Science and Christian Theology on Human Origins: An 'Aesthetic Supralapsarianism.'" *Perspectives on Science and Christian Faith* 62 (2010): 196–212.

Christ's atonement. This questioning of the biblical Adam not only undermines the doctrine of original sin, but also the notion of Christ's atonement as a payment for human sin. If Christ has not paid for our sins, how are we to be saved? Since God is now responsible for sin, Schneider favors a universalism where God, in His love, saves all humans. This, however, contradicts the biblical teaching of divine judgment and eternal punishment for unbelievers (Revelation 20:12–15; Matthew 13:36–43). God is not only love, but also just.

Also, Paul's comparison of the first Adam to the second Adam (Christ) loses its force if the first Adam never really existed. Then we need another account of how man fell into sin. Indeed, we would also need another explanation for the traditional Christian view of the atonement.

Why did Jesus have to die? The Bible says that death was the result of sin (Romans 5:12). If human death occurred before Adam, then physical death is not a penalty for sin, thus directly contradicting Scripture (e.g., Roman 3:23–25; 1 Peter 3:18). Then there is no explanation or justification for the sacrificial system, and there remains no valid biblical explanation for why Jesus had to die.[24] Joseph Bankard, adapting the Bible to evolution, contends that Christ came to show us the nature of God, to serve as an example to us, and that his death was not part of God's plan, since God's forgiveness doesn't require blood.[25] This clashes with the words of Peter: *"this Jesus, delivered up according to the definite plan… of God"* (Acts 2:23).

The historicity of the biblical Adam is therefore a significant issue affecting many Christian doctrines.

---

24 Roger Birch, "Why Did Jesus Die? The Sacrificial System and Creation." *Salt Shakers Journal,* 15 (November 2009): 3–5.

25 Joseph Bankard, "Substitutionary Atonement and Evolution, Part 2." *BioLogos,* June 10, 2015 (http://biologos.org/blog/substitutionary-atonement-and-evolution-part-2).

4.3 EVALUATING THE SCIENTIFIC EVIDENCE

How strong is the scientific case for human evolution? It is based primarily on fossil and genetic evidence. Let's briefly examine these evidences.

Fossil evidence. Ideally, if humans evolved from ape-like creatures, one would expect to find a series of ancient fossils reflecting a gradual change from ape-like to human. This, however, is not the case.

One difficulty is that hominid (ancient ape- or human-like) fossils are very rare, often consisting of mere bone fragments.

A further problem is that hominid fossils do not show a gradual transition from ape-like to human-like. Rather, *Homo erectus* fossils, which are very similar to modern humans, appear abruptly about two million years ago, according to mainstream dates.[26] The evolutionary biologist Ernst Mayr commented,

> *The earliest fossils of Homo, Homo rudolfensis and Homo erectus, are separated from Australopithecus by a large, unbridged gap. How can we explain this seeming saltation? Not having any fossils that can serve as missing links, we have to fall back on the time-honored method of historical science, the construction of a historical narrative.*[27]

The fossil evidence is generally problematic for macroevolution. Listen again to Ernst Mayr:

> *Given the fact of evolution, one would expect the fossils to document a gradual steady change from ancestral forms to the descendants. But this is not what the palaeontologists finds [sic]. Instead, he or she finds gaps in just about every phyletic series.*[28]

---

26 For more on this, read *Science & Human Origins*, by Ann Gauger, Douglas Axe, and Casey Luskin (Seattle, WA: Discovery Institute, 2012).

27 Ernst Mayr, *What Makes Biology Unique?* (Cambridge, UK: Cambridge University Press, 2004), 198.

28 Ernst Mayr, *What Evolution Is* (New York, NY: Basic Books, 2001), 14.

Most fossil species appear suddenly, fully formed, and then remain virtually unchanged until they disappear. Gradual change from one species to another is not observed.

Genetic evidence. Given the shortcomings of fossil evidence, the case for human evolution relies mostly on genetic evidence.

Central to genetics is DNA (deoxyribonucleic acid), the molecule found in the nucleus of about seventy-five percent of all cells; the human body has about one hundred trillion cells.[29] It determines how an organism develops. DNA contains many genes, which are molecular codes for making everything an organism needs, especially proteins. Proteins are large biological molecules that perform various functions within the cell. Humans have about twenty-five thousand genes in each DNA molecule. Genes are packaged in groups called chromosomes.

The human genome is a complete copy of the entire set of gene instructions. Humans have twenty-three pairs of chromosomes (each chromosome has one copy from each parent). Our offspring get a random selection from each pair of these chromosomes.

In reproduction, the cell needs to make copies of its DNA. Sometimes a copying mistake is made in the sequence of the DNA. This is called a mutation. Evolution assumes that random mutations cause changes in organisms, and that natural selection will weed out bad mutations and further propagate good mutations. In this way, life allegedly evolved from a simple cell to more complicated organisms, and eventually to humans.[30]

Comparing the DNA of various species may thus give important evidence of evolution. Similarities and differences in DNA may indicate how closely related various species are to each other.

---

29 Mature red blood cells, which constitute about twenty-five percent of our one hundred trillion cells do not have a nucleus. See: "Red blood cell," *Wikipedia.* Date of access: September 23, 2015 (https://en.wikipedia.org/wiki/Red_blood_cell).

30 As noted earlier, macroevolution has never been observed in a laboratory. If mutations are to be the engine for macroevolution, they must be radially function-gaining, able to create a new genome from scratch, yet none exist.

A. SIMILARITY OF HUMANS AND CHIMPANZEES.

The human genome is closest to that of chimpanzees. How close? Some say that they differ by only about one percent. This is taken as evidence that humans and chimpanzees have a common ancestor.

However, the differences are actual much larger. This one percent figure is based on comparing only those stretches of chimp DNA that are similar to human DNA. It ignores those parts of the DNA that are dissimilar.[31]

For example, one study found that many genes in chimps differ totally from those in humans.[32] The study infers that since the presumed split of humans from chimps, humans gained 689 new genes whereas chimps gained 729 different genes. Thus, merely in terms of genes, humans differ by at least six percent ([689+729]/23,000=0.062).

Further, the actual genes make up only a few percent of the genome. The rest of the genome is concerned with regulating the genes, turning on switches, and other functions that are not yet fully understood. When the total genome is taken into account, the difference between chimps and humans increases to about twenty percent.[33]

However, even if humans and chimps are genetically similar, this does not demonstrate common ancestry. Genetic similarity between humans and chimps could be a result of common design. Since humans and chimps have similar bodies, parts of which have similar functions, they need similar proteins. Hence, one would expect that many genes would be very similar.

---

31 Don Cohen, "Relative Differences: The Myth of 1%." *Science*, 316 (June 29, 2007) 1836.

32 Jeffery P. Demuth, Tijl De Bie, Jason E. Stajich, Nello Cristianini, Matthew W. Hahn, "The Evolution of Mammalian Gene Families." *PLoS One* 1 (December 20, 2006): e85.

33 Jeffrey Tomkins and Jerry Bergman, "Genomic Monkey Business—Estimates of Nearly Identical Human-Chimp DNA Similarity Re-Evaluated Using Omitted Data," *Journal of Creation* 26 (April 2012): 94–100.

B. SEQUENCES OF GENES AND PSEUDO-GENES.

Further evidence for evolution comes by comparing similar genes and pseudo-genes (parts of the genome that appear to be genes that have lost their function). By comparing similar genes of various animals, it is thought possible to determine a gene's hereditary line. For most genes, humans are closest to chimps. If humans and chimps actually evolved from a common ancestor, one might expect that chimps would be closest for all similar genes. However, this is not the case; fifteen percent of human genes are closer to gorillas than to chimps.[34] This undermines the notion that humans evolved from chimps.

C. "ORPHAN" GENES.

Many genes in humans have no similar counterpart among apes. Hence, they are called "orphan" genes, since they appear to have no ancestors. As we saw above, humans have 689 orphan genes that are said to have originated after the presumed human-chimp split. These are hard to explain via evolution, which views human genes as modified versions of ancestor genes. The development of an entirely new gene calls for a complete set of scores of good mutations, which has an extremely low probability.

D. EVIDENCE AGAINST AN INITIAL PAIR.

Thus far we have shown that the scientific evidence for human evolution from ape-like creatures is not clear-cut; furthermore, it can be interpreted in terms of common design.

What about the evidence for the notion that humans could not have originated from a single pair?

This claim is based on the currently observed genetic diversity among humans. Humans all have very similar DNA: 99.9% is the same. It is assumed that all diversity comes from random mutations operating

---

34 Kerri Smith, "Gorilla Joins the Genome Club." *Nature,* March 7, 2012 (http://www.nature.com/news/gorilla-joins-the-genome-club-1.10185).

on an initially common genome. Estimates of at least ten thousand humans at any time are based on idealized statistical models using assumed mutation rates, random breeding, no migrations, and so on.

However, several recent studies cast doubt on the reliability of these estimates. Genetic diversity is not necessarily higher in a larger population.[35] In cases where the initial population size was known (e.g., Mouflon sheep and Przewalski's horses), the genetic diversity many generations later was found to be much greater than expected on the basis of the models.[36]

Geneticist Robert Carter has shown that the genetic data can readily be interpreted in ways consistent with an initial human pair—the biblical Adam and Eve.[37] For example, our DNA has two copies (one from each parent) of each chromosome but one. Our offspring get a random combination of these chromosomes. If Adam had two different forms of many genes, rather than two identical copies of each, this could explain the human genetic diversity, since most genes have only two different forms.

5. CHRONOLOGY: WHEN WAS ADAM?

Thus far we have argued for the necessity and scientific viability of the biblical Adam and Eve, the first humans, ancestors of all other humans past and present.

Many Christians, although accepting the biblical Adam, still believe that mainstream fossil dates are correct. This view is called old-earth creationism (OEC). But how does the biblical Adam fit into mainstream chronology?

---

35 Hans Ellegrin, "Is Genetic Diversity Really Higher in Large Populations?" *Journal of Biology* 8 (2009): 41.

36 Fazale Rana, "Who was Adam?" in *More than Myth?* P.D. Brown and R. Stackpole, eds. (Seattle, WA: Chartwell Press, 2014), 165.

37 Robert Carter, "The Non-Mythical Adam and Eve," *Creation.com.* August 20, 2011 (http://creation.com/historical-adam-biologos).

Mainstream science gives the following chronology of human history:[38]

2,500,000 B.C.:	first tool-making hominins (*Homo*).
2,000,000 B.C.:	*Homo erectus*, anatomically very similar to modern man.
200,000 B.C.:	emergence of *Homo sapiens* and Neanderthals.
50–40,000 B.C.:	oldest artistic and religious artifacts.
40,000 B.C.:	first aborigines in Australia, continuously there since.
9000 B.C.:	first villages.
7500 B.C.:	first plant cultivation, domesticated cattle and sheep.
5000 B.C.:	first bronze tools.
3000 B.C.:	first written records.
1600 B.C.:	first iron tools.

5.1 AN ANCIENT ADAM IN MAINSTREAM CHRONOLOGY

If Adam was the first human, he should precede the first human-like fossil, dated about two million B.C., according to mainstream dates.

This contradicts the traditional biblical chronology, which puts the creation of Adam and Eve at about 4000 B.C. According to the genealogies of Genesis 5 and 11, Adam was 130 years old when he fathered Seth, Seth was 105 when he fathered Enosh, and so on. Adding up the ages of the fathers at the births of their named sons, this gives about two thousand years from Adam to Abraham, who lived about two thousand years before Christ. This puts Adam at about 4000 B.C.

Such a date, based on the Genesis genealogies, was accepted by virtually all Christians (including Jerome, Augustine, Luther, and Calvin)

---

38 As typified by Brian M. Fagan, *People of the Earth: An Introduction to World Pre-History*, 13th ed. (New York, NY: Pearson Publisher, 2009).

until the 1860s.[39] Then, for the first time, large gaps in the genealogies were postulated to bring Adam's date in line with the mainstream scientific chronology.

Whether the Bible allows for any gaps is dubious,[40] but stretching the genealogies from two thousand years to two million years—a factor of more than one thousand—certainly seems implausible.

There is a further difficulty. The biblical Adam and Eve were not primitive, naked hunter-gathers dwelling in caves. Rather, they were intelligent, had sophisticated language, and were clothed. Adam was a gardener. His son Abel was a shepherd, and his son Cain was a farmer, a *"worker of the ground"* who founded a city (Genesis 4). Tents, musical instruments, and bronze and iron tools were all invented a few generations later by Cain's offspring (Genesis 4). This description of Adam places him much more recently, at about 10,000 BC, according to mainstream chronology.

5.2 A RECENT ADAM IN MAINSTREAM CHRONOLOGY

Accordingly, some Christians who accept mainstream chronology have opted for a recent Adam.

Unhappily for these Christians, this creates other problems. For example, mainstream chronology places aborigines in Australia continuously for the last forty thousand years. Hence, if Adam lived at 10,000 B.C., then today's Australian aborigines could not be descendants of Adam.

This raises the question of whether the aborigines bear the image of God, and if so, whether they are tainted by Adam's sin. Original sin was traditionally considered to have been propagated in a hereditary manner from Adam to all his posterity. How then does original sin affect

---

39 Ian T. Taylor, *In the Minds of Men: Darwin and the New World Order*, 6th ed. (Foley: MN, TFE Publishing, 2008), 362.

40 We note that some young-earth creationists (YEC) hold that the Genesis genealogies may contain gaps, extending the creation date of Adam up to 10,000 B.C. For further details, see David Mcgee, "Creation Date of Adam from the Perspective of Young-Earth Creationism," *Answers Research Journal* 5 (November 2012): 217–230.

the aborigines? Further, Christ's atonement is a penal substitution where Christ, as a representative descendant of Adam, pays for the sins of Adam's race. How can aborigines share in this if they are not descendants of Adam?

5.3 A MEDIUM-AGED ADAM IN MAINSTREAM CHRONOLOGY

For the above reasons, most Christians embracing mainstream chronology place Adam somewhere between 200,000 B.C. and 40,000 B.C. (a "medium-aged" Adam). Hugh Ross dates Adam at about 50,000 BC,[41] and theologian Millard Erickson places Adam at about 30,000 BC, with the presumed beginning of language and growth of culture.[42]

This entails rejecting the detailed description of Adam and his sons as given in Genesis 4, as well as the genealogies of Genesis 5 and 11.

A further problem concerns older human lookalikes dating back two million years. The close similarity between these ancient fossils and modern humans strongly suggests that Adam had human-like ancestors. Or did God create humans twice?

Fazale Rana dates Adam at about 40,000 B.C., with the appearance of sophisticated tools and art. He considers Adam and Eve the first creatures that bore God's image. All other human-like creatures, both before and after Adam, were mere animals that became extinct.[43] Adam, though virtually identical in DNA to his human-like neighbors, is said to differ in rationality, behavior, and communication skills. Is that plausible? Were human-like creatures among the beasts named by Adam?

Mainstream neuroscience claims that spiritual properties (thinking, willing, feeling) are all products of the brain, which is in turn determined by genetics. On that basis, one might expect Adam's DNA to differ significantly from that of his soulless lookalikes.

---

41 Hugh Ross, *More than a Theory* (Grand Rapids: MI, Baker Books, 2009), 190.

42 Millard J. Erickson, *Christian Theology* (Grand Rapids, MI: Baker Academic), 2013. Chapter 22.

43 Fazale Rana, "Who was Adam?" in *More than Myth?* P.D. Brown and R. Stackpole, eds. (Seattle, WA: Chartwell Press, 2014), 157–175.

Paul specified, *"For not all flesh is the same, but there is one kind for humans, another for animals, another for birds, and another for fish"* (1 Corinthians 15:39). If hominid flesh is identical to human flesh, should they then not be considered humans?

In sum, the biblical Adam cannot be placed within mainstream chronology without rejecting major portions of Genesis 1–11.

6. THE ORIGIN OF NATURAL EVIL

How can we account for natural evil such as earthquakes, disease, suffering, predation, and biological death? Traditionally, Christians believed that God created the world *"very good"* (Genesis 1:31). All natural evil was caused by Adam's fall, which brought about a drastic corruption of nature.

This view has recently been endorsed by theologian Wayne Grudem,[44] but it clashes with his earlier acceptance of mainstream chronology.[45] According to mainstream chronology, ancient fossils indicate that natural evil existed long before Adam.

Consequently, many Christians believe that Adam's fall did not have any observable effects. They limit the fall primarily to making Adam liable to *spiritual* death. Natural evil is then seen as part of God's "very good" creation, making God responsible for it.

Some hold that suffering, disease, and death are necessary byproducts in a universe created by God to evolve moral agents with genuine freedom.[46] Others, not wanting to hold God responsible for natural evil, contend either that animals do not really suffer, or that natural evil, before the fall of Adam, is due to satanic corruption.[47]

---

44 Wayne Grudem, "Foreword" in *Should Christians Embrace Evolution?* Norman C. Nevin, ed. (Nottingham, UK: InterVarsity Press, 2009).

45 Wayne Grudem, *Systematic Theology* (Leicester, UK: InterVarsity Press, 1995), 279.

46 R.J. Russell, *Cosmology* (Minneapolis, MN: Fortress, 2008), 221.

47 C.S. Lewis, *The Problem of Pain* (New York, NY: MacMillan Publishing, 1962), 135; Gregory Boyd, *Satan and the Problem of Evil* (Downers Grove, IL: IVP Academic, 2001).

In contrast, the Bible attributes the curse on the earth (Genesis 3:17; Genesis 5:29) to the sin of Adam, not angels. The curse affected plants (Genesis 3:18) and animals (Genesis 3:14). Compare Genesis 1:31 (*"And God saw everything that he had made, and behold, it was very good"*), before the fall, with Genesis 6:12 (*"And God saw the earth, and behold, it was corrupt, for all flesh had corrupted their way on the earth"*). The corruption is associated with violence, and all flesh here includes the animals.

In the future, Christ will bring about a renewal, a restoration to a very good state (e.g., Romans 8:18–25, 2 Peter 3:5–13, 1 Corinthians 15:21–26). The entire earth will be cleansed from evil, the result of Adam's sin. The drastic nature of this cleansing, comparable to the Flood, suggests that the fall and the Flood both resulted in great changes in creation.

Is biological death fundamental to life on this earth? Christian evolutionary biologist Jeffrey Schloss disputes this:

> *At the organismal level, there are no physiological or thermodynamic reasons why death must occur. In fact, there are several unicellular species that are immortal and one advanced multicellular organism (Bristlecone Pine) that has not demonstrated any signs of senescence (i.e., aging). The evolutionary interpretation of senescence is not that it represents biological failure or necessity, but is an adaptation built in to organisms, enhancing fitness by "making room" for progeny.*[48]

It is biologically conceivable that all natural evil is due to the post-fall corruption of a previously innocent creation that initially contained no suffering, animal death, or predation.

The traditional biblical explanation of the existence of natural evil is therefore a further reason to question mainstream chronology.

---

48 Jeffrey P. Schloss, "From Evolution to Eschatology," in *Resurrection: Theological and Scientific Assessments*, T. Peters, ed. (Grand Rapids, MI: Eerdmans, 2002), 83.

If Adam, the first human, was created recently, then mainstream dates for the earliest human-like fossils (two million years ago) must be erroneous.

How well-established are mainstream fossil dates?

Fossil dates are based primarily on radiometric methods. Consider, for example, carbon dating.[49] It is used to date once-living organic remains of animals or plants, such as bones, flesh, or wood.

Radioactive carbon-14 is constantly formed in the atmosphere by the interaction of cosmic rays with atmospheric nitrogen. Plants absorb carbon (C-14 and normal C-12) from the atmosphere by photosynthesis; animals absorb carbon by eating plants. After death, the C-14 decays with a half-life of about 5,700 years to nitrogen-14, thus changing the C-14 to C-12 ratio over time. Eventually, all the carbon that remains will be C-12. By measuring the ratio of C-14 to C-12 in a sample, and knowing the initial ratio at death, one can estimate the time since death.

However, the atmospheric ratio of C-14 to C-12 is not constant. It is affected by volcanic eruptions, changes in cosmic ray intensity, the earth's magnetic field, etc. Hence, carbon dates must first be calibrated using known dates. Further, not all animals get their carbon from the usual food chain, yielding strange results (e.g., a living snail in Italy was dated at 2,100 years old[50]). Calibrated carbon dating works best for ages up to about five thousand years. Theoretically, it can be used up to fifty thousand years, but the reliability is much lower. C-14 should not be measurable in remains older than one hundred thousand years (but see below for contrary evidences).

Older fossils are dated in terms of overlying lava flows, using other radiometric methods. For example, when lava solidifies from a molten state, any potassium (K) in it will decay to argon (Ar), with a half-life of 1.2 billion years. By measuring the ratio of K to Ar, the age of the lava

---

49 For example, see John Morris, *The Young Earth* (Green Forest, AR: Master Books, 2007), 63–67.

50 G. Quarta et al, "Radiocarbon Age Anomalies in Pre- and Post-Bomb Land Snails." *Radiocarbon* 49 (2007): 817–826.

is estimated. This assumes that the decay is constant, that there is no initial Ar, and that no K or Ar leaves or enters the lava. All other dating techniques depend on similar assumptions.

Here, too, anomalous results have been found; for example, basalt from the 1959 eruption of Kilauea Iki in Hawaii was dated at 8.5±6.8 million years ago.[51] Such anomalous results are generally explained away in terms of mainstream science. Nevertheless, this cautions us about simply accepting mainstream chronology at face value, particularly when historical records cannot verify it.

Further, there are various phenomena that challenge mainstream chronology. For example, C-14 has been found in coal and diamonds, all of which are allegedly millions or billions of years old, and thus should contain no C-14.[52]

Also, preserved soft tissue and blood vessels from various dinosaurs have been found.[53] Since such organic remains usually decompose in the order of thousands of years, this presents a serious challenge to the mainstream view that dinosaurs died off sixty-five million years ago.

On such grounds, one can question the reliability of mainstream chronology.

8. CHRONOLOGY: THE GENESIS DAYS

Another controversial issue concerns the creation days of Genesis 1. Are these real days, long ages, or merely metaphorical poetry?

Favoring literal days is the fact that the creation "day" is defined as a period of light, followed by "night," a period of darkness (Genesis

---

51 D. Krummenacher, "Isotopic Composition of Argon in Modern Surface Volcanic Rocks." *Earth and Planetary Science Letters* 8 (1970): 109–117.

52 J. Baumgardner, in *Radioisotopes and the Age of the Earth*, L. Vardiman, A. Snelling, and E. Chaffin, eds. (El Cajon, CA: Institute for Creation Research, 2005), 587–632.

53 M. Schweitzer et al., "Soft-Tissue Vessels and Cellular Preservation." *Tyrannosaurus Rex, Science* 307 (2005): 1952–1955. Also see: M.H. Armitage et al., "Soft Sheets of Fibrillar Bone from a Fossil of the Supraorbital Horn of the Dinosaur Triceratops horridus." *ActaHistochemica* 115 (July 2013): 603–608.

1:5). The sun is created on Day 4 to rule the day (Genesis 1:16). Thus, the last three days are certainly solar days. Further, the Sabbath (Day 7) was a real day, since it was blessed, and set the pattern for the following Sabbaths (Exodus 31:12–18).

It is noteworthy that many Christian theologians and philosophers grant that the literal view is exegetically preferred, but nevertheless reject it because they are convinced of the truth of mainstream chronology (e.g., J.P. Moreland[54] and Gleason Archer[55]).

How about the day-age view, where each day corresponds to an era of millions of years?[56] Aside from the exegetical shortcomings just noted, the *order* of events presents a challenge. For example, the Genesis account follows this order: grasses and fruit trees (Day 3), the sun (Day 4), fish, whales, and birds (Day 5), land mammals and reptiles (Day 6). Mainstream science, on the other hand, follows this order: the sun (five billion years ago), fish (500 million years ago), reptiles (360 mya), mammals (200 mya), birds (150 mya), grasses and fruit trees (70 mya), and whales (40 mya).[57] The day-age view thus satisfies neither sound exegesis nor mainstream chronology.

Accordingly, to accommodate mainstream science, it has become popular among theologians to take Genesis 1 to be a literary framework, with metaphorical days.[58] As such, its message is mainly theological, declaring that God created the entire universe. A clash with

---

54 J.P. Moreland, *Scaling the Secular City* (Grand Rapids, MI: Baker Books, 1998), 219–20.

55 Gleason Archer, *A Survey of Old Testament Introduction* (Chicago, IL: Moody Press, 1994), 196.

56 Hugh Ross, "Genesis 1 and Science," in *More than Myth*, P.D. Brown & R. Stackpole, eds. (Seattle, WA: Chartwell Press, 2014).

57 Extracts from Jeffrey Bennett et al., *Cosmic Perspective*, 3rd ed. (San Francisco, CA: Benjamin Cummings, 2005); Collin Renfrew and Paul Bahn, *Archaeology*, 3rd ed. (New York, NY: Thames and Hudson, 2000); "Timeline of the Evolutionary History of Life," *Wikipedia*, Date of access: September 23, 2015 (https://en.wikipedia.org/wiki/Timeline_of_the_evolutionary_history_of_life).

58 Bruce K. Waltke, *Genesis* (Grand Rapids, MI: Zondervan, 2001), 61.

mainstream science is avoided by emptying Genesis 1 of any specific historical information.

Whether Genesis 1 has a clearly defined literary structure is debatable. A number of possible literary structures have been proposed. None of these gives an exact fit with the actual text.[59] In fact, the most obvious pattern is the traditional "six days plus one" (Exodus 20:8–11) view.

Even if Genesis 1 were to display a highly stylized literary form, why should that diminish its historicity? This is a false dilemma, because Genesis could be *both* well-written and factually correct. God created according to His perfect plan; hence, His work should exhibit perfect structure.

Finally, as we saw above, accepting the biblical Adam already puts one at odds with mainstream chronology. Hence, it is pointless to revise Genesis 1 without doing the same for Genesis 2–11.

9. GOD'S TWO BOOKS

It is often said that God reveals truth through two books: His Word (special revelation) and His works (general revelation). Since God is the author of both, they cannot contradict each other. Hence, the argument goes, any apparent contradiction must be due to our misinterpretation of either Scripture or nature. Generally, it is Scripture that ends up being reinterpreted.

In support of this, reference is often made to texts such as:

For his invisible attributes, namely, his eternal power and divine nature, have been clearly perceived, ever since the creation of the world, in the things that have been made. So they are without excuse. (Romans 1:20)
The heavens declare the glory of God... (Psalm 19:1)

---

59 Paulin Bedard, *In Six Days God Created* (Maitland, FL: Xulon Press, 2013).

Note, however, that nature's message here concerns only the knowledge of God—namely, God's eternal power and deity. Moreover, nature's message is so immediate and clear that everyone is *"without excuse."* There is no need of special scientific knowledge. It seems that God has created us with an innate sense enabling us to clearly discern God's glory in nature.

If nature is to be viewed as a book, it is a special type of a book. Nature, unlike the Bible, is not a book containing propositional truth. Rather, it is a picture book, where the letters are creatures and things (i.e., people, animals, birds, insects, mountains, seas, trees, stars, etc.)

Since nature has existed since before Adam, the book of nature covers all of history. Yet the only pages we can now read are those pertaining to today, circa A.D. 2000. Those pages tell us nothing about biblical history, which begins at creation (about 4000 B.C.) and stops toward the end of the first century A.D. There is thus no direct conflict between biblical history and the current chapter of the book of nature.

One must not confuse nature with science, our fallible human effort to understand nature. The Bible is the testimony of the Creator Himself regarding truth that is inherently inaccessible to human perception and inquiry. Hence, we should read the book of nature using the spectacles of Scripture.

10. CONCLUSIONS

10.1 WHY ARE CHRISTIANS DIVIDED OVER ORIGINS?

Divisions over origins are caused by mistaken confidence in scientific claims that, for example, miracles are impossible, that humans evolved from ape-like creatures, or that the earth is billions of years old.

Yet in science we must always distinguish between (1) actual observations and (2) their theoretical explanation. The above claims are not based upon clear-cut empirical evidence, but upon philosophical assumptions.

Such claims come from a naturalistic version of science. Naturalism is the dominant worldview in today's Western secularized society.

Evolution seems proven because it is the only view allowed in public media, education, and academia. The case for evolution is made to seem much stronger than it really is.

10.2 A CLASH OF WORLDVIEWS

The controversy regarding origins is primarily a clash of worldviews. Christians believe that the Bible, as the Word of God, gives a true account of historical events. They believe that reality is much greater and richer than the visible physical world.

Mainstream science, on the other hand, ignores God and His Word, and tries to explain everything in terms of purely natural causes.

Theistic evolutionists and old-earth creationists accept mainstream astronomy, geology, and biology to varying degrees and then reinterpret Scripture accordingly. Such a syncretistic mix of Christian and naturalist premises compromises one's basic faith in God's Word.

This book's two appendices will assist the reader in further understanding the various positions held on origins in terms of key premises, features, and notable influencers.

10.3 THE NEED FOR CONSISTENCY

Worldviews come as package deals; they are all-encompassing systems. One cannot simply mix and match. Compromising Christianity with naturalism introduces a logical inconsistency that will eventually undermine our commitment to God and His Word. We saw, for example, the dire consequences for Christian doctrine if there was no biblical Adam. At stake are such issues as biblical clarity, authority and inerrancy, original sin, and Christ's atonement.

We must therefore be consistent in our faith. If we cannot believe *everything* the Bible affirms, how can we believe *anything* in it? Where do we draw the line? How do we justify any reduction in biblical authority? If taking the Bible at face value is simplistic, what alternative hermeneutics must be applied? And how is this to be biblically justified?

In short, either we believe the entire Bible, interpreted in its plain sense, or we don't. Belief in the Bible as God's Word entails that we accept the traditional, plain-sense view of the Bible on origins.

10.4 HANDLING SCIENTIFIC EVIDENCE

How then should we approach scientific evidence?

1. We should be aware of weaknesses in evolutionary explanations.
2. We should be aware of the presuppositions, limitations, and implications of naturalistic science.
3. We should develop alternative Bible-based historical science. Various creationist models have been developed in astronomy,[60] geology,[61] and biology.[62] These models address such issues as light from distant galaxies, the big bang theory, the origin of life theories, Darwinian natural selection, the fossil order, genetics, and large radiometric "dates" within biblical parameters, among many others. (See Resource section.)

We do not know what processes God used during the creation week, nor what the finished universe looked like on the seventh day. It may well have had a great apparent age, if examined in terms of naturalistic assumptions. Also, we do not know the full extent of changes in the universe caused by the fall or the Flood.

---

60 For example, J. Harnett, *Starlight, Time and the New Physics* (Eight Mile Plains, AU: Creation Book Publishers, 2007); J. Byl, *God and Cosmos* (Carlisle, PA: The Banner of Truth Trust, 2001).

61 For example, A. Snelling, *Earth's Catastrophic Past: Geology, Creation & the Flood* (Dallas, TX: ICR, 2009). Available as two volumes.

62 For example, Kurt P. Wise, *Faith, Form, and Time* (Nashville, TN: Broadman & Holman, 2009); Paul Garner, *The New Creationism* (Orpington, UK: Grace Publishing, 2009); and Todd Charles Wood, *Animal and Plant Baramins* (Eugene, OR: Wipf & Stock Publisher, 2008).

Although creationist models can be useful in showing how scientific data could be interpreted to be consistent with the Bible, we should be careful never to use these to prove the Bible to be true. The presumed truth of the Bible is our starting point, not our conclusion; *the truth of the Bible does not depend on our fallible scientific models.* Indeed, any discrepancy between our scientific reconstruction of history and biblical history can always be attributed to some deficiency in our scientific assumptions.

Finally, we humbly plead with you to carefully consider your position on origins, for the Lord's sake. Enter into a new stage of radical biblical faith that places God's Word as your primary guide to faith and practice. We live in an exciting age that intersects our biblical faith with science, where the *"harvest is plentiful, but the laborers are few. Therefore pray earnestly to the Lord of the harvest to send out laborers into his harvest"* (Luke 10:2).

> *Do not be conformed to this world, but be transformed by the renewal of your mind, that by testing you may discern what is the will of God, what is good and acceptable and perfect. (Romans 12:2)*

 # APPENDIX 1: COMPARISON OF VARIOUS POSITIONS HELD ON ORIGINS

Legend:

YEC: Young-Earth Creationism
OEC: Old-Earth Creationism
GT: Gap Theory
TE: Theistic Evolution
LF: Literary Framework
DE: Deistic Evolution
AE: Atheistic Evolution

| YEC | OEC (+ GT) |
	TE (+ LF) DE AE
► Genesis 1–11 is historical narrative, not to be reinterpreted by science.	► Genesis 1–11 is not historical narrative and/or must be reconciled with mainstream science.
	► Genesis 1–11 is ancient myth.
INFLUENCE OF MAINSTREAM SCIENCE: "SCIENCE RECONCILES OR REINTERPRETS SCRIPTURE" (using theologians/scientists/philosophers/etc.)	
► NEVER	► OFTEN ► ALWAYS
OVERALL VIEW OF SCIENCE (versus Scripture)	
► Lower	► Higher ► Highest
OVERALL VIEW OF SCRIPTURE	
► Highest (no compromise)	► Mixed ► Lowest (compromise) (irrelevant)

KEY FEATURES OF THE "GREAT DIVIDE" IN THE TABLE:

YEC: Maintains tradition biblical view and modifies science accordingly. It includes a plain historical narrative interpretation of early Genesis and biblical Adam, a young universe/earth (thousands of years old), no macroevolution, and worldwide Noahic flood.

OEC: Allows for an ancient universe and earth (millions/billions of years, or "deep time"), but insists that God created the various "kinds" directly, including Adam and Eve. It includes no macroevolution, no worldwide flood, and allows death before Adam and the fall.

GT: An interpretive device held by some OECs, which allows a gap between Genesis 1:1–1:2 to accommodate modern geological deep time. Its theology is refuted today by nearly all Old Testament scholars

TE: Allows macroevolution, death before Adam and Eve, an ancient universe and earth (deep time), and doesn't allow for a global flood. This is also known as evolutionary creation.

LF: Popular interpretive device used in a broad spectrum of non-YEC views. It assumes that Genesis 1 is figurative or symbolic, accepts deep time and macroevolution, and differs little from TE. There are many types: revelatory, Ancient Near East, cosmic temple, analogical, etc.

APPENDIX 2: FURTHER DETAILS ON POSITIONS HELD ON ORIGINS

Position	Key Premise/ Bias	Main Features	Notable Influencers
YEC	Scripture leads	no macroevolution; death begins at Adam's fall due to sin; young universe/earth, global flood	Martin Luther, John Calvin, Louis Berkhof, John MacArthur, D. James Kennedy, Douglas F. Kelly, Robert McCabe, Terry Mortenson, Henry Morris, Ken Ham, Carl Wieland, J. Sarfati
OEC	Science integrated with Scripture	no macroevolution; old universe and earth; no global flood; death before Adam and the fall	Walter Kaiser, Hugh Ross, Gleason Archer, Millard Erickson, Wayne Grudem, Davis Young, Norman Geisler, Lee Strobel, William Lane Craig, J.P. Moreland, John C. Lennox

Position	Key Premise/ Bias	Main Features	Notable Influencers
GT	Science leads	similar to OEC; GT now refuted	Thomas Chalmers (1814), Scofield Reference Bible (1917), A. Custance, John Sailhamer (modified GT)
TE	Science leads	macroevolution; old universe and earth; no global flood; death before Adam and the fall	Asa Gray (1840), Howard J. Van Till, Francis Collins, Darrel Falk, Kenneth R. Miller, Bruce Waltke, Peter Enns, Denis O. Lamoureux, Karl W. Giberson, Timothy Keller
LF	Theological framework leads	non-committal to above views, but closest to TE; Genesis days are only figurative or symbolic	Arie Noordtzij (1924), Meredith G. Kline, Ronald F. Youngblood, P.J. Wiseman, C. John Collins, John Walton
DE	Science only (after God started everything)	closest to TE; macroevolution (needs old age); no global flood; death before Adam and the fall	David Hume (1760), Jean Lamarck (1780), James Hutton (1790), Charles Lyell (1830), Charles Darwin (1870)
AE	Science only	naturalism (materialism) is everything; basis of mainstream science; old universe/earth; macroevolution; (myth) death before Adam/the fall	Anthony Flew (pre-2006), Isaac Asimov, Francis Crick, Louis/Mary Leakey, Stephen Jay Gould, Stephen Hawking, Richard Dawkins

RESOURCES

Here are some recommended resources to answer questions the reader may have.

1. What is intelligent design?[63]

Dembski, William A. and Sean McDowell. *Understanding Intelligent Design: Everything You Need to Know in Plain Language.* Eugene, OR: Harvest House Publishers, 2008.

Dembski, William A. and Jonathan Wells. *The Design of Life: Discovering Signs of Intelligence in Biological Systems.* Dallas, TX: Foundation for Thought and Ethics, 2008.

Website: (Uncommon Descent)

2. What is wrong with the evolution paradigm today?

Ashton, John F. *Evolution Impossible: 12 Reasons Why Evolution Cannot Explain the Origin of Life on Earth.* Green Forest, AR: Master Books, 2012.

Batten, Donald et al. *Evolution's Achilles' Heels,* R. Carter, ed. Powder Springs, GA: Creation Book, 2014.

Johnson, Phillip E. *Defeating Darwinism by Opening Minds.* Downers Grove, IL: InterVarsity Press, 1997.

Lennox, John C. *God's Undertaker: Has Science Buried God?* Oxford, UK: Lion, 2009.

Taylor, Ian T. *In the Minds of Men: Darwin and the New World Order.* 6th ed. Foley, MN: TFE Publishing, 2008.

3. What is wrong with theistic evolution?

Norman C. Nevin, ed. *Should Christians Embrace Evolution? Biblical and Scientific Responses.* Phillipsburg, NJ: P&R Publishing, 2011.

Otis, John M. *Theistic Evolution: A Sinful Compromise.* Burlington, NC: Triumphant Publications, 2013.

4. What is wrong with old-earth creationism?

Mortenson, Terry. *The Great Turning Point: The Church's Catastrophic Mistake on Geology—Before Darwin.* Green Forest, AR: Master Books, 2004.

Sarfati, Jonathan. *Refuting Compromise.* Green Forest, AR: Master Books, 2004.

5. What is wrong with big bang cosmology? How do you explain distant starlight in a young universe?

Byl, John. *God and Cosmos: A Christian View of Time, Space, and the Universe.* Edinburgh, UK: The Banner of Truth Trust, 2001.

Hartnett, John. *Starlight, Time and the New Physics.* Atlanta, GA: Creation Book, 2007.

---

63 The proponents of intelligent design (ID) contend that the universe shows evidence of design by a Creator, versus naturalistic science. Many are OEC or TE, and generally avoid discussing the Bible. ID is primarily a science-related strategy for reaching academia.

Williams, Alex and John Hartnett. *Dismantling the Big Bang: God's Universe Rediscovered.* Green Forest, AR: Master Books, 2005.

6. How do you explain the geological evidence for a young earth?

Garner, Paul. *The New Creationism: Building Scientific Theory on a Biblical Foundation.* Welwyn Garden City, UK: Evangelical Press, 2009.
Oard, Mike and John K. Reed, eds. *Rock Solid Answers: The Biblical Truth behind 14 Geological Questions.* Chino Valley, AZ: Creation Research Society, 2009.
Snelling, Andrew. *Earth's Catastrophic Past: Geology, Creation and the Flood.* Dallas, TX: ICR, 2009.

7. How do you explain the biological/fossil evidence versus evolution?

Gauger, Ann, Douglas Axe, and Casey Luskin. *Science & Human Origins,* Seattle, WA: Discovery Institute, 2012.
Lubenow, Marvin L. *Bones of Contention: A Creationist Assessment of Human Fossils.* Grand Rapids, MI: Baker Book, 2004.
Sanford, J.C. *Genetic Entropy & the Mystery of the Genome,* 2nd ed. Lima, NY: Elim Publishing, 2008.
Wise, Kurt P. *Faith, Form, and Time: What the Bible Teaches and Science Confirms about Creation and the Age of the Universe.* Nashville, TN: Broadman & Holman Publishers, 2002.
Wood, Todd. *Animal and Plant Baramins.* Eugene, OR: Wipf & Stock, 2008.

8. How does a Christian worldview differ from naturalism?

Byl, John. *The Divine Challenge: on Matter, Mind, Math and Meaning.* Edinburgh, UK: The Banner of Truth Trust, 2004.

9. How should we read Genesis?

Kelly, Douglas F. *Creation and Change: Genesis 1.1–2.4 in the Light of Changing Scientific Paradigms.* Fearn, UK: Christian Focus Publications Ltd., 1997.
Kulikovsky, Andrew S. *Creation, Fall, Restoration: A Biblical Theology of Creation.* Fearn, UK: Christian Focus Publications Ltd., 2009.
MacArthur, John. *The Battle for the Beginning: Creation, Evolution, and the Bible—The Bible on Creation and the Fall of Adam.* Nashville, TN: Thomas Nelson Books, 2001.
Mortenson, Terry and Thane H. Ury, eds. *Coming to Grips with Genesis: Biblical Authority and the Age of the Earth.* Green Forest, AR: Master Books, 2008.
Sarfati, Jonathan D. *The Genesis Account: A Theological, Historical, and Scientific Commentary on Genesis 1–11.* Powder Springs, GA: Creation Book Publishers, 2015.

Do you have further questions? These sites address many questions on Christianity and origins:

www.creation.com (Creation Ministries International)
www.icr.org (Institute for Creation Research)
www.answersingenesis.org (Answers in Genesis)
www.bylogos.blogspot.ca (John Byl)